Designing a
Shuttle

Elisa Jordan, M.A.

✳ Smithsonian

T0027312

Contributing Author

Heather Schultz, M.A.

Consultants

Dr. Valerie Neal
Space History Curator
National Air and Space Museum

Tamleka Grizzle, Ed.D.
K–5 STEM Lab Instructor
Harmony Leland Elementary School

Stephanie Anastasopoulos, M.Ed.
TOSA, STREAM Integration
Solana Beach School District

Publishing Credits

Rachelle Cracchiolo, M.S.Ed., *Publisher*
Conni Medina, M.A.Ed., *Managing Editor*
Diana Kenney, M.A.Ed., NBCT, *Series Developer*
June Kikuchi, *Content Director*
Véronique Bos, *Creative Director*
Robin Erickson, *Art Director*
Seth Rogers, *Editor*
Mindy Duits, *Senior Graphic Designer*
Smithsonian Science Education Center

Image Credits: front cover, p.1 NASA/Kim Shiflett; pp.2–3, p.4, p.5 (all), p.7 (bottom), p.10 (all), p.11 (bottom), p.12, p.13 (bottom right and left), p.14 (all); p.16 (left); p.17 (all), p.18 (all), p.19, p.20 (all), p.21 (top), p.22, p.23 (all), p.24 (all), p.25 (all), 26 (right), p.31, p.32 (all) NASA; p.6 (left) British Library Board/ Bridgeman Images; p.7 (top) Sheila Terry/Science Source; p.8 (right), p.9 (bottom right) RIA Novosti/ Science Source; p.9 (top) Richard Bizley/Science Source; p.9 (bottom left) Bastetamon/Shutterstock; p.11 (top) Lee Aucoin; p.15, p.16 (right), p.26 (left), 27 (top left) © Smithsonian; p.27 (top right) NASA/Paul E. Alers; p.27 (bottom) NASA/Smithsonian; all other images from iStock and/or Shutterstock

Library of Congress Cataloging-in-Publication Data

Names: Jordan, Elisa, author.
Title: Designing a shuttle / Elisa Jordan.
Description: Huntington Beach, CA : Teacher Created Materials, Inc., [2018] |
Audience: Grades 4 to 6. | Includes index. | Description based on print
version record and CIP data provided by publisher; resource not viewed.
Identifiers: LCCN 2018005459 (print) | LCCN 2018008920 (ebook) | ISBN
9781493869411 (E-book) | ISBN 9781493867011 (pbk.)
Subjects: LCSH: Space shuttles--Juvenile literature. | Space vehicles--Design
and construction--Juvenile literature. | Aerospace engineering--Juvenile
literature.
Classification: LCC TL795.515 (ebook) | LCC TL795.515 .J67 2018 (print) | DDC
629.47/4--dc23
LC record available at https://lccn.loc.gov/2018005459

Smithsonian

Teacher Created Materials

5301 Oceanus Drive
Huntington Beach, CA 92649-1030
www.tcmpub.com
ISBN 978-1-4938-6701-1

Table of Contents

Introducing the Space Shuttle!

In the early 1970s, the United States was the world leader in space travel. Americans landed men on the moon six times. The National Aeronautics and Space Administration (NASA) wanted to make more trips into space. But flying to space was expensive. Each trip used a new spacecraft. When a ship came back to Earth, it crashed into the ocean. It could not be used again.

NASA wanted to build a new kind of spacecraft. Its goal was to design a craft that could be used over and over again. This would save money and make it easier to bring people and equipment to and from space. This goal turned into NASA's space shuttle program.

The space shuttle program came out of years of research. It took a long time for people and rockets to start launching people into space. Scientists and engineers had to figure things out one step at a time. Luckily, they had a long history to build on.

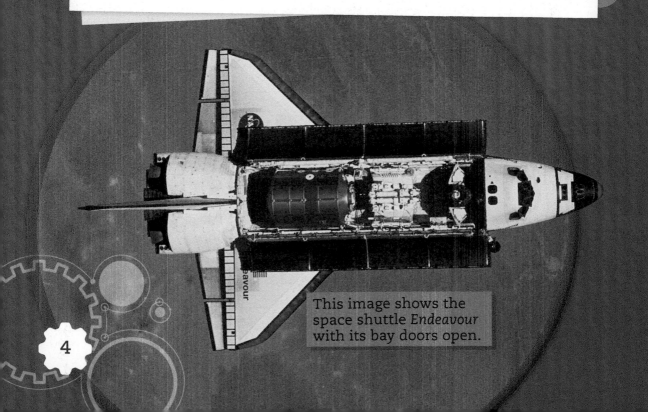

This image shows the space shuttle *Endeavour* with its bay doors open.

4

Apollo 16 launches in 1972.

Mercury's *Friendship 7* launches in 1962.

A single rocket launch in the 1960s cost NASA up to $175 million.

Long Ago

No one knows when the Chinese discovered the recipe for **gunpowder**. Around the year 900, they learned that if they made a small change to the recipe, gunpowder would burn instead of explode. This mixture was first put in bags tied to arrows. The arrows burned whatever they hit.

After a while, the bags were replaced with tubes. This changed everything. When the gunpowder burned, it pushed the arrow forward. The arrow flew farther. They didn't know it then, but these were the first rockets.

gunpowder

This print shows Chinese soldiers with flaming arrows.

Four hundred years later, Galileo Galilei (ga-lih-LEY-oh ga-lih-LEY) used a telescope to look into the night sky. This allowed him to see distant stars and planets more clearly. People used telescopes to learn more about the **solar system** and Earth's place in it. The dream to fly to these places was not long off.

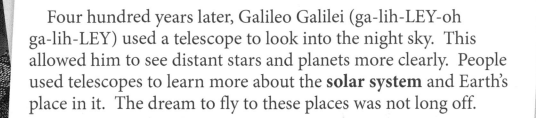

1891 woodcut of Galileo

SCIENCE

Rocket Science

Rockets create **thrust** by burning fuel in a mostly sealed container. When fuel is burned, it turns into a gas and expands. Because it is in a sealed container, it can only escape from one place. Gas passes through a nozzle that helps control the rocket's direction. As gas escapes in that direction, the rocket moves in the opposite direction.

Space Race

By the 1950s, scientists and engineers in the Soviet Union and the United States learned a lot about rockets. The two countries were rivals. They did not share data. People in each country wanted to prove their technical abilities.

In 1957, the team from the Soviet Union surprised the world when it put a **satellite** into orbit. The team from the United States worked hard to catch up. They wanted to be the world leader in space. Four years later, the Soviets struck first again when they sent a man into space. President John F. Kennedy challenged NASA to have an American walk on the moon before 1970. In July 1969, they did. The Soviets could not keep up. This was the end of the space race.

The space race taught scientists a lot. They knew astronauts could spend time in space safely. Research in space was now possible. The space shuttle program was started so NASA could send people into space more often. Rockets were expensive and could only be used one time. A new spacecraft that could be used over and over again would let NASA fly into space more often.

Over five hundred people have been to space. Of them, 355 rode on a space shuttle at least once.

Yuri Gagarin was the first man in space.

This illustration shows *Vostok 1*, the craft that carried Gagarin.

This is a replica of *Sputnik 1*, the first satellite in orbit.

Vostok 1 after it landed on Earth

Designing the Space Shuttle

Once NASA decided to send people to space on shuttles, scientists and engineers had to design them. There were many questions that needed answers. What does a space shuttle look like? Would it have wings like an airplane? How would it carry enough fuel? How would it return to Earth?

The team started to work on shuttles in 1972. The first space shuttle didn't launch until 1981. It took a long time to figure out how to make the ideas work for a real spacecraft.

First, scientists had to figure out everything a space shuttle needed to do. A space shuttle had to be strong enough to survive a launch into outer space. But it also needed to be light enough to fly. Astronauts were going to stay onboard. A shuttle had to be large enough to be their home. They were also going to work in the space shuttle. A lab had to be part of the design.

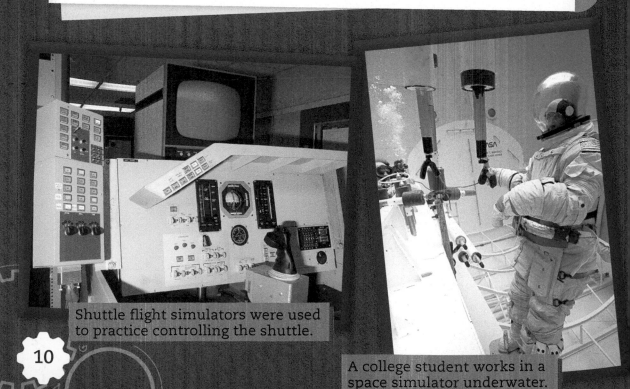

Shuttle flight simulators were used to practice controlling the shuttle.

A college student works in a space simulator underwater.

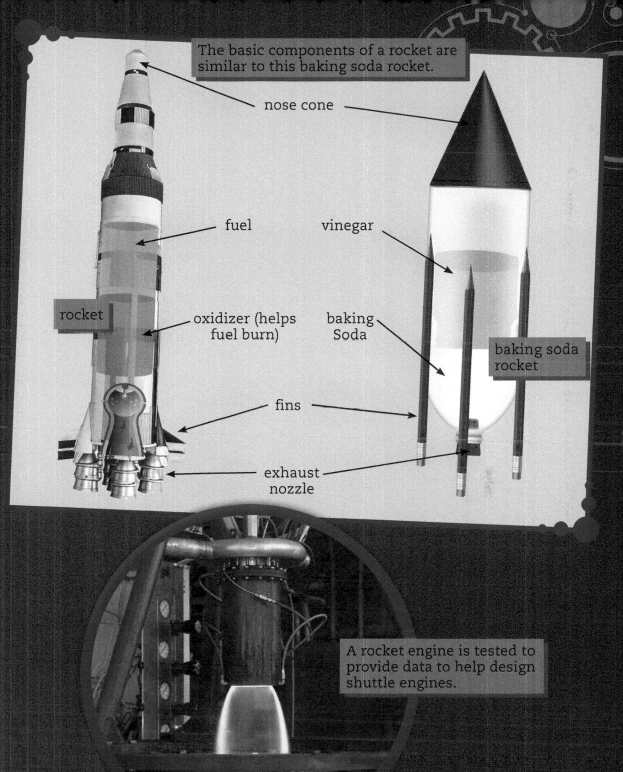

The basic components of a rocket are similar to this baking soda rocket.

nose cone

fuel

vinegar

rocket

oxidizer (helps fuel burn)

baking Soda

baking soda rocket

fins

exhaust nozzle

A rocket engine is tested to provide data to help design shuttle engines.

Hot Topic

The team thought about many details. Engineers started drawing what a space shuttle might look like. The first designs looked like an airplane. But airplanes are not meant to fly outside of Earth's stratosphere. The shuttle would need an outside rocket system to get it past the stratosphere. External tanks would hold the fuel and oxygen the shuttle would need. So, the shuttle became a glider. A NASA team also realized that the shuttle had to **withstand** extreme heat. Some materials change shape when they get hot. This is called thermal distortion. It is what happens when shuttles reach the thermosphere.

Scientists found that shuttle bay doors were affected by thermal distortion. Engineers figured out how to make bay doors that would not break when flying through the thermosphere. They added special closures. They made the doors more **flexible**. They could hold up to changing temperatures and still function.

shuttle bay doors

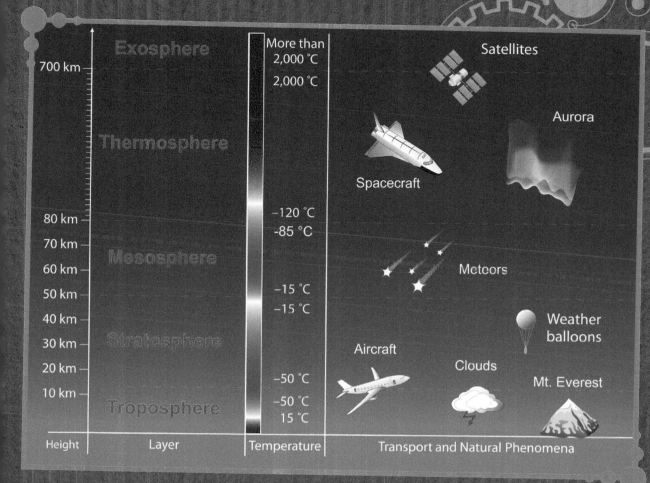

Height	Layer	Temperature	Transport and Natural Phenomena

Exosphere

700 km

Thermosphere

More than 2,000 °C

2,000 °C

Satellites

Spacecraft

Aurora

80 km
70 km
60 km
50 km
40 km
30 km
20 km
10 km

Mesosphere

Stratosphere

Troposphere

−120 °C
-85 °C

−15 °C
−15 °C

−50 °C

−50 °C
15 °C

Meteors

Weather balloons

Aircraft

Clouds

Mt. Everest

Glenn in 1962

John Glenn orbited Earth in 1962. In 1998 he flew in space again when 77 years old, making him the oldest person ever in space.

Glenn in 1998

13

Next, engineers had to figure out how to make the whole space shuttle withstand heat and be flexible, too. They had to design a cover that would flex but not break. This cover is called the skin. Since the shuttle would be used again, the skin needed to be strong and able to withstand high temperatures.

Silica tiles are cut to fit like a skin.

Tiles are tested in ovens to learn how they work during re-entry.

The design team thought of many ideas. They had to choose which idea would work best. They finally decided that small tiles made of silica would work. Silica is found in sand and in quartz. It is used to make glass. The small tiles allowed the shuttle's body to flex during launch or in space if it needed to. One large skin would crack. So more than 25,000 smaller silica tiles were used!

Heat shield tiles cover most of a space shuttle.

Scientists and engineers look at more than 20 different weather conditions including temperature and cloud cover to decide whether a launch can happen.

Combining New and Old

A lot of new ideas were used to build the space shuttle. But engineers also relied on some old ideas. **Aluminum** is a material used to build airplanes. Engineers decided to use it on the shuttle because it is strong. It is also lightweight and flexible.

Traveling in space shuttles is not the same as on airplanes. People stay in seats on airplanes. When they get up, they can walk around. But in space, people float! This can make even simple tasks much more difficult.

An astronaut eats in space.

shuttle toilet

The scientists and engineers who designed the shuttle made sure astronauts had places to sleep. Like people on Earth, astronauts need to sleep at least eight hours. If astronauts don't want to bump into things while they are sleeping, they have to attach themselves to something. There were beds and sleeping bags for them. They could also sleep sitting in their seats.

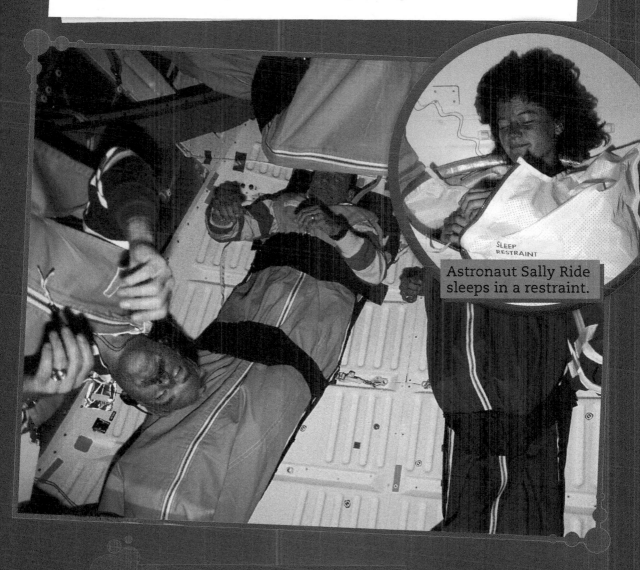

Astronaut Sally Ride sleeps in a restraint.

The engineers and scientists who designed the shuttle created something completely new. But it took them many tries. They had to think of many ideas. Then, they had to test those ideas. Even if the tests were successful, they often made improvements to the designs. Sometimes, they had to start over! After all their tests, the space shuttle had three main parts.

The first part of a space shuttle is called the **orbiter**. This part looks like an airplane. It is the only part of the shuttle that launches into space. The second part is called the external tank. It is a large fuel tank attached to the orbiter. It provides fuel to the engines. The third part of the shuttle is the **solid rocket booster**. There are usually two of them. They are tall, skinny rockets on both sides of the orbiter. The boosters are the engines that help push the orbiter off the ground and into the air.

In 1980, engineers inspect the shuttle bay doors of *Columbia* as they open for the first time.

An engineer tests a shuttle model in a wind tunnel.

external tank

NASA's space shuttle was
56 meters (184 feet) long. It
weighed 2 million kilograms
(4.5 million pounds).

orbiter

solid rocket
booster

Shuttle Missions

The first space shuttle mission took place in 1981. It was very exciting to see its launch after years of hard work! The space shuttle could carry seven people. Astronauts had a lot of work to do. They studied many things, such as gravity and weightlessness. Scientists wanted to see how **cells** change in new places. Seeing how cells change helps scientists understand how cells work. That can lead to better medicines.

Astronauts also studied how liquids act in space. Gravity changes many of the properties of liquids on Earth. In space, liquid forms spheres. Boiling water on Earth causes bubbles to rise to the surface of the water. In space, the lesser effect of gravity means gas will not rise to the top when liquids boil. Instead, bubbles just grow larger and larger at the heat source.

A drop of soda forms a sphere while in space.

John W. Young and Robert L. Crippen were the first two astronauts to fly in a shuttle.

Space shuttle *Columbia* launches in 1981.

Medical Breakthrough

Astronauts tested *Salmonella* bacteria on the space shuttle. People can get very sick from it on Earth. In space, the bacteria got stronger. Scientists believed this happened because space "tricked" it. The bacteria thought it was inside a person's body. Scientists watched it and did tests. They invented a vaccine to help people get better on Earth.

There were 135 space shuttle missions from 1981 to 2011. One of the most important goals of the program was to build the International Space Station (ISS). The ISS is very big. In fact, it's the largest object ever flown in space. Sometimes, people can see it from Earth.

The United States and 15 other countries helped build the ISS. It orbits Earth 16 times per day. Astronauts from around the world live and work on the ISS, usually in crews of six, so they can learn more about space. Some of the space shuttle's missions were to add or repair parts on the ISS.

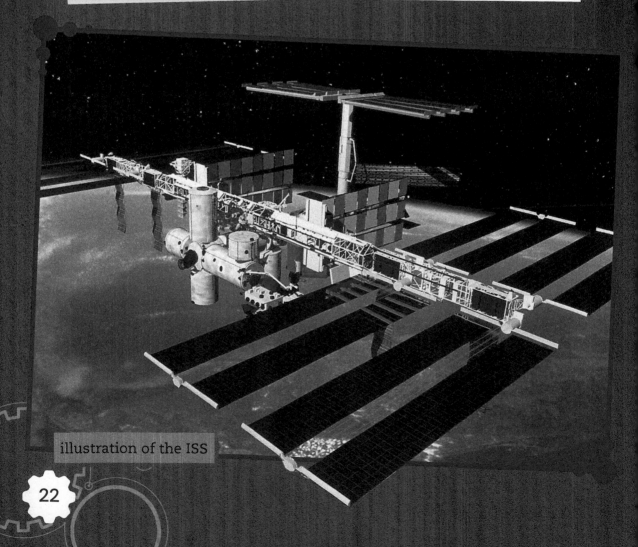
illustration of the ISS

The space shuttle also launched the Hubble Telescope. It can see a lot! It has made more than a million observations since it launched. Like any piece of equipment, the Hubble sometimes needs to be fixed. The space shuttle crew repaired and updated it during five service missions.

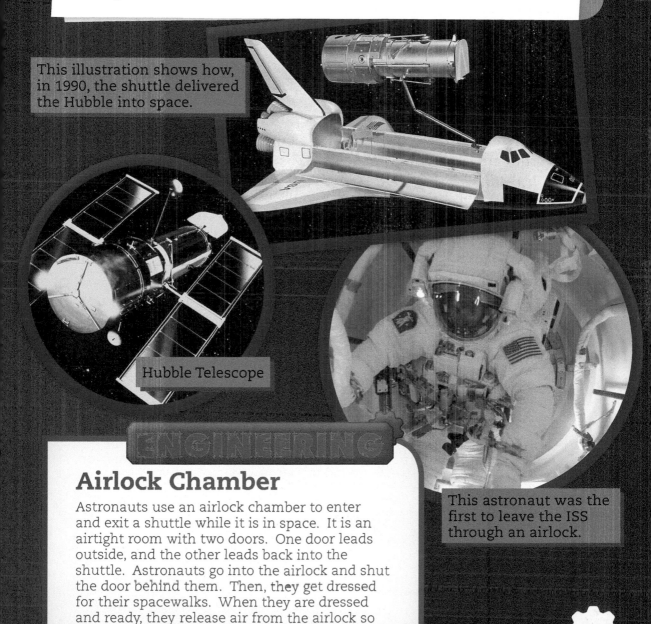

This illustration shows how, in 1990, the shuttle delivered the Hubble into space.

Hubble Telescope

ENGINEERING

Airlock Chamber

Astronauts use an airlock chamber to enter and exit a shuttle while it is in space. It is an airtight room with two doors. One door leads outside, and the other leads back into the shuttle. Astronauts go into the airlock and shut the door behind them. Then, they get dressed for their spacewalks. When they are dressed and ready, they release air from the airlock so they can open the door that leads outside.

This astronaut was the first to leave the ISS through an airlock.

Legacy of the Space Shuttle

In the past, explorers traveled on land to see what was beyond the **horizon**. Then, they traveled by sea to see what was across the oceans. Astronauts are explorers, too. They want to see what is beyond our planet.

NASA wanted to honor the explorations of the past. It named all the shuttles after ships whose voyages helped make many discoveries in science.

The first space shuttle was named *Enterprise*. It never flew in space. The first shuttle to go to space was *Columbia*. The space shuttles after that were *Challenger*, *Discovery*, *Atlantis*, and *Endeavour*. All the space shuttles discovered new things about science just like the ships they were named after.

Thanks to the space shuttle program, we know a lot more about space flight. The program expanded the range of useful activities that people can do in space. They also built better equipment and spaces where astronauts can live and work.

The original *Star Trek* television series called space the "final frontier." It is! There is still so much to explore in space.

Columbia lands after its first mission in 1981.

Challenger lands after a 1985 mission.

The crew of *Discovery* pose for a photo in 2000.

This is an image of *Endeavour* taken from the ISS in 2009.

ARTS

Choosing the Delta Wing

A space shuttle is like a rocket, but it is also like an airplane. Look closely—there are differences between the wings of most planes and space shuttles. Some airplanes have straight wings. Shuttles have **delta wings**. Engineers used delta wings on the shuttle because they produce more lift to glide longer. This allows the shuttle to move more easily. Also, vehicles with delta wings do not heat up as much when they come back to Earth.

straight-wing orbiter concept

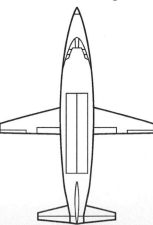

delta-wing orbiter concept

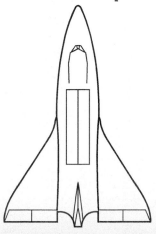

NASA ended the space shuttle program after 30 years and 135 missions. The program was supposed to last for 15 years. But it lasted twice as long. It was time to try something new.

Overall, the program was a success. But there were two shuttle accidents. One shuttle broke apart right after takeoff. Another broke apart 16 minutes before landing. Sadly, the crew members of both missions did not survive.

When the space shuttle program ended, NASA had four space shuttles left. These space shuttles are part of history. No one wanted to destroy them. Where could they go? Four museums around the country became their new homes.

One space shuttle is displayed at Smithsonian's National Air and Space Museum. Another is at a museum in New York City. A third shuttle is now at a science center in Los Angeles. The last one is at the Kennedy Space Center in Florida. Visitors can now see these amazing shuttles in person!

An astronaut stands on the flight deck of *Discovery*.

The last shuttle flight carried a large container of student experiments.

Discovery lands after its final mission.

Enterprise is flown to a New York airport.

Discovery

Enterprise

MATHEMATICS

Shuttles by the Numbers

During the program's 135 missions, the space shuttles did many things. They carried over 1,500 tons of cargo into space. They spent a total of 1,323 days in space and orbited Earth 20,830 times.

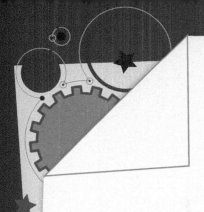

STEAM CHALLENGE

Define the Problem

An engineer's first design is rarely the best solution to a problem. When designing something as large as a space shuttle, engineers often make small models to test their designs. Your task is to build a model shuttle that can be successfully launched with a straw.

 Constraints: Your model may only use one sheet of paper and tape.

 Criteria: The paper shuttle must go at least 1 meter (1 yard) when launched by blowing through a straw.

Research and Brainstorm

What wing shape will work best? How many wings will work best? Where should the wings be placed? What forces are acting on your shuttle?

Design and Build

Sketch your design including measurements for each part of your model shuttle. Build the model.

Test and Improve

Launch your paper shuttle from your straw three times. Did your shuttle go 1 m (1 yd.) or more? Did your shuttle design provide consistent results? Get feedback. Modify your design and try again.

Reflect and Share

What factors affected your shuttle's flight pattern? How can you minimize the effects of these factors? Will other types of materials improve the results?

Glossary

aluminum—a type of shiny, silver metal that comes in many forms, such as foil

cells—the basic building blocks of all living things

delta wings—triangular, swept-back wings

flexible—able to be bent

gunpowder—an explosive mixture used in guns and explosives

horizon—the line where the sky seems to meet the earth or sea

orbiter—the part of the space shuttle that went into space and looks like an airplane

satellite—a machine that is launched into space and moves around Earth or another body in space

solar system—a star with bodies, such as moons and planets, revolving around it

solid rocket booster—a solid fuel engine that helped push the orbiter into space

thrust—the force that drives something forward

withstand—to stand against or resist

Index

Do you want a career in space?
Here are some tips to get you started.

"NASA hires people with many different interests. I started out writing about science and technology for NASA. Whatever you like to do, there is a future space career for you!" —*Dr. Valerie Neal, Space History Curator*

"Museums are committed to teaching and inspiring students. Visit as many air and space museums as possible. Learn about spacecraft by listening to museum guides. They are experts in their field. They can help you find where your passion lies." —*General John "Jack" Dailey, former National Air and Space Museum Director*